HAMLYN - COLOURMAX

RIDING

JULIA GOODWIN

CONTENTS	
Starting Out	2
Types of Horses	4
Features of the Horse	6
Your First Lesson	8
Mastering the Basics	10
Your Pony's Paces	12
Improving Your Technique	14
Learning to Jump	16
Feeding	18
Grooming	20
Tack 1	22
Tack 2	24
Buying/Borrowing a Pony	26
What Next?	28
Competing	30
Index	32

HAMLYN

STARTING OUT

WHERE SHOULD I RIDE?

Finding a riding school that suits you is a vital first step once you have been bitten by the horse and pony bug! Riding schools vary a great deal. Beginners do not need all the facilities that a large riding school charges for. It might be worth starting with a smaller school and moving on as you gain more experience. Schools are listed in your local telephone directory.

Before you make a final choice, arrange to visit the schools you think are possibles. If you turn up casually the staff may be too busy to show you around, but if you make an appointment you should be welcomed and allowed to look round freely. Reputable riding schools are licensed by their local authority. The certificate should be displayed in the office.

WHAT TO LOOK FOR

Do not expect to see brand new stables and equipment. Instead, look for signs that the yard and ponies are clean and well cared for. The ponies should look well-fed, healthy and reasonably contented. Widespread coughing, sticking out ribs or any saddle sores on ponies in work are bad signs.

The ponies should have access to clean water and the bedding should be ample and clean. There should be no dangerous tools, such as pitchforks, left lying in the yard and fencing round fields and paddocks should be safe and secure. Ask how many pupils will be in your lesson and if there are helpers on the ground in addition to the class instructor.

Try to watch a lesson. An indoor arena is ideal, as you can ride whatever the weather, but these are expensive and not all schools can afford them. However, there should be a properly fenced outdoor arena of roughly 40 × 20 metres. You should see letter markers and some dismantled jumps for use in more advanced lessons. All the pupils should be wearing proper hats and sensible shoes, if not riding boots.

Below: A well-maintained riding school.

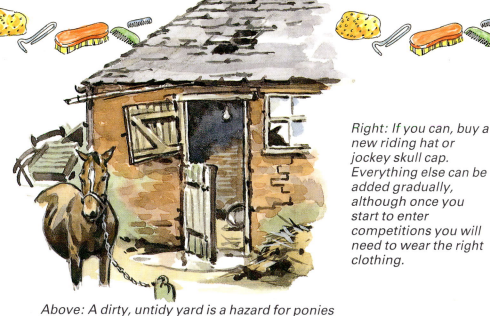

Above: A dirty, untidy yard is a hazard for ponies and riders. Nor should ponies be chained up.

Right: If you can, buy a new riding hat or jockey skull cap. Everything else can be added gradually, although once you start to enter competitions you will need to wear the right clothing.

WHAT TO WEAR

You can spend a small fortune on riding clothes! But to begin with you can manage with a few essentials, adding gradually to your basic kit and saving up for good leather riding boots or a smart tweed jacket.

The most important item in your riding kit will be your hat. For your first lesson you will probably be able to borrow one from the school, but if you intend to continue with your new hobby you should soon buy one of your own.

There are two types: a jockey skullcap, which conforms to British Standard 4472, and a traditional riding hat which conforms to BS 6473. Both have permanent chinstraps that will keep the hat firmly on your head if you have a fall. It is worth investing in a new hat; you do not know how many knocks a second-hand hat has been subjected to and these will weaken the structure.

You will also need sturdy shoes with a small heel – wellington boots or flat trainers will just slip through the stirrup. Rubber riding boots are reasonably inexpensive and they will protect your legs. You will also need a pair of comfortable, loose trousers (not tight jeans) and a jumper which allows you to move your chest and shoulders comfortably. A waterproof jacket is a wise investment, as is a pair of cotton string gloves – they will stop your hands slipping on the reins.

Left: This is the correct turnout for gymkhana, hunter trial, show and showjumping classes.

TYPES OF HORSES

There are hundreds of different breeds of horses and ponies throughout the world. The two which have dominated internationally are the Thoroughbred and Arab.

Above: A Thoroughbred.
Right: An Arab shows how gracefully he moves.

THOROUGHBRED
Thoroughbreds are the fastest horses in the world. Although their origins stem from Arab blood, they have been crossed with many other breeds to give them extra speed. Thoroughbreds can be any colour except piebald and skewbald. Height 15.2 hands average, but some may be as big as 17 hands.

ARAB
Arabs are the oldest pure breed of horse. They have had the biggest influence on all other breeds throughout the world. Arabs are thought to date back to 5000 BC when they

roamed wild in the Yemen. Arabs have dished (concave) faces and are fast and full of stamina. Arabs can be bay, chestnut or grey. Height 14.2–15 hands.

WHAT WILL I RIDE?
Most of the ponies at a riding school are a mixture of several breeds. They are chosen because they have a quiet nature and are easy to ride.

COLOURS
Bay and brown are the most common colours, but not all ponies are the colour they appear! If in doubt look at the "points" of the pony – mane, tail, eye rims and muzzle. Some animals change colour over the years: greys become lighter as they get older and white Lippizaners are born black.

1 Yellow Dun
Golden with black points. A Blue Dun has a blackish coat with black points
2 Bay
Brown with black points
3 Brown
Brown
4 Palomino
Golden with white mane and tail
5 Black
Black
6 Strawberry Roan
Chestnut and white hairs. A Blue Roan has black and white hairs
7 Skewbald
Large patches of white and any other colour except black
8 Grey
Black and white hairs. Dapple greys have large round rings on their coats, flea bitten greys have small flecks of black on their coats
9 Piebald
Large black and white patches
10 Chestnut
Red-brown

FEATURES OF THE HORSE

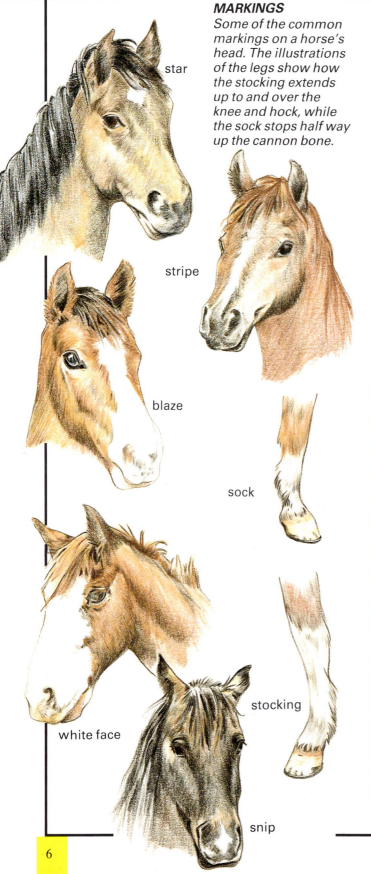

MARKINGS
Some of the common markings on a horse's head. The illustrations of the legs show how the stocking extends up to and over the knee and hock, while the sock stops half way up the cannon bone.

POINTS OF A HORSE
As soon as you start to ride, your instructor will refer to the different parts of your horse, using phrases such as "Keep your hands off the withers" and "Leg on the girth". Try to learn the names and positions of the "points" of a horse.

1 cheek
2 chin groove
3 muzzle
4 nostril
5 forelock
6 poll
7 ear
8 mane

Try to learn a few points of the horse every day. Start at his head and gradually work your way round his body. Understanding how your pony's body is made up will make you a better rider.

9 withers	23 fetlock joint
10 back	24 stifle
11 croup	25 sheath
12 hindquarter	26 flank
13 dock	27 ribs
14 tail	28 belly
15 thigh	29 elbow
16 point of hock	30 chestnut
17 hock	31 cannon
18 fetlock	32 knee
19 heel	33 forearm
20 coronet	34 breast
21 hoof	35 shoulder
22 pastern	36 neck

HEIGHT

Ponies are measured in hands, from the ground to the top of the withers. One hand is 10 cms. If the measurement is less than 14.2 hands high, the animal is called a pony. Any animal bigger than this is a horse.

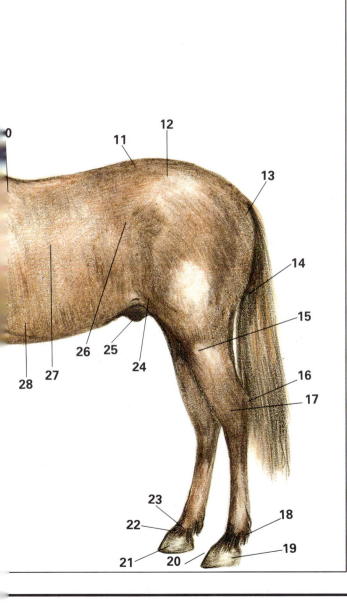

SEX

Mare – female horse or pony over four years old.
Stallion – male horse over four years old.
Filly – young female horse or pony under four.
Colt – young male horse or pony under four.
Gelding – castrated male horse or pony.
Foal – young horse under one year.
Yearling – young horse or pony between one and two years old.

YOUR FIRST LESSON

At your first lesson make sure you arrive at the stables in plenty of time so you can watch other people handling and riding the ponies. Spend a few minutes patting your horse's neck and saying "hello" to him before you get on his back. The instructor will tighten the girth before you mount, so the saddle does not slip. He will do this on the horse's near (left) side. This is the side from which you will mount. The right-hand side is called the off-side.

MOUNTING

1 Check the girths are tight. Stand to the left of the pony, with your left shoulder next to the pony's neck and hold the reins loosely in your left hand. Put your left foot in the stirrup: hold it towards you with your right hand. Try not to prod the pony with your toe! This is the sign for him to move forward.

2 Hold the front of the saddle with your right hand and spring up off the ground.

3 Swing your right leg over the pony's back being careful not to kick him. Lower yourself gently into the saddle. Put your right foot in the stirrup.

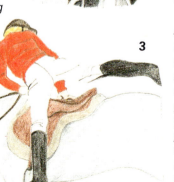

DISMOUNTING

1 Take both feet out of the stirrups. Hold your pony's neck and reins firmly in your left hand and the front of the saddle with your right.
2 Lean forward and lift your right leg over the pony's back so you can jump down on to the pony's near side. Make sure you don't kick him with your leg.
3 Bring your legs together and slip to the ground. Run the stirrup irons up inside the leathers so they rest against the saddle. Take the reins over the pony's head and lead him to the stable or field.

ADJUSTING THE STIRRUPS

Once in the saddle, your stirrups will need adjusting to the correct length. Lift the saddle flap, pull the stirrup leather up against the buckle and move it up or down. Repeat with the other stirrup. To check the length, take your feet out of the stirrups. Your ankle should touch the bottom of the iron.

ADJUSTING THE GIRTH

Move your leg forwards and lift the saddle flap. Tighten the girth strap gradually otherwise you will pinch your pony. Check that you can fit two fingers between the girth and your pony.

REMEMBER

Never approach a pony without warning him of your presence; he will bolt at any unusual or startling noise, or if anything creeps up on him silently. Murmur a word or two to let him know you are close by.

Sound confident. If you sound terrified as you approach, he will become nervous too.

Never walk too close behind a horse. If he is frightened he may kick you – hard!

Always wear a hard hat when you go riding.

Above: If you perch in the saddle you will have no control over your pony. Also, if he stops or changes direction suddenly you will fall off.

Right: To sit correctly, sink your weight into the saddle and imagine a straight line through your ear, shoulder, elbow, hip and ankle.

IN THE SADDLE

When your pony first moves off, try to relax. Sit in the central lowest part of the saddle. Do not slump forward, but avoid being so stiff that you tip backwards.

Check that each side of your body is level; try not to twist to either side or to lean too far over as this will throw your pony off balance.

Relax your arms and shoulders; if they are too stiff they will pull on the reins. Do not rest your hands on his neck or hold them up too high. Keep your legs close to the girth, with your toes pointing straight ahead and your heels below the level of your toes. Sit up straight, shoulders back and chin raised.

Mastering the Basics

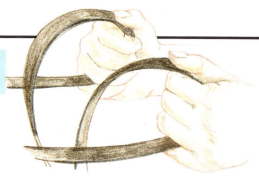

Holding the reins
The reins should thread between your third and fourth fingers. Keep your thumbs on top, and your wrists and elbows in a straight line with the reins, your wrists rounded towards each other.

Moving off
When you want to walk forward straighten your back and gently squeeze both legs firmly against your pony's sides. Keep a light contact with his mouth and follow the movement of his head and neck with your hands as he moves off. Do not pull on the reins.

Turning
Move one hand slightly away from your pony's neck in the direction you wish to follow. Keep your other hand close to your pony's neck to stop him turning too far. At the same time your inside leg should be close against the girth, while your outside leg slides back behind the girth and squeezes against your pony's side.

Stopping
To stop from a walk, sit deep in the saddle and squeeze your knees. Close your hands on the reins, release and close again. Also, close your calves against the pony's sides.

A LUNGE LESSON
The best place to learn to ride is in a lunge lesson. It teaches you to sit correctly in the saddle from the start. The instructor stands in the centre of the arena holding a lunge rein attached to your pony's noseband. The instructor controls the pony's speed and direction so you can concentrate on your position in the saddle.

Lunge lessons are strenuous so they are usually limited to 30 minutes. Your pony will be tired afterwards and your muscles will ache the following day. While you are on the lunge you will probably carry out a series of exercises designed to improve your balance and boost your confidence.

Below: During a lunge lesson, the instructor controls the pony so you can concentrate on keeping your balance and riding correctly.

EXERCISING IN THE SADDLE
Arm circling
Rotate one arm slowly backwards in large circles. Repeat with the other arm. This opens up your chest and strengthens your shoulders.

Legs away
Hold the front of the saddle with both hands, then lift both legs away from your pony's sides, keeping your knees bent. This stretches your thigh muscles and will help you to sit more deeply in the saddle.

Round the world
Swing your left leg over the front of the saddle so you are sitting sideways. Next swing your right leg over the back. Bring your left leg over the back, then swing your right leg over your pony's withers so you are back in the correct position. This exercise will improve your balance.

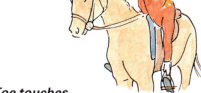

Toe touches
Reach down and touch your left toe with your left hand. Then your right toe with your right hand. Then touch alternate toes. This is good for your waist and balance.

RIDING AIDS
Aids are the signals used to tell a pony what he should do. Signals using different parts of the body – your legs, hands, seat, back and voice – are called "natural" aids. More experienced riders sometimes use "artificial" aids such as whips and spurs.

Legs
A pony's instinct tells him to move away from pressure on his sides, so your legs can either push a pony forwards or ask him to stop. Your legs should normally be on the girth. When you turn or canter, your outside leg moves behind the girth. When you want your pony to change pace, close your legs against his sides. This warns him something is about to happen. If you want to go faster, close your legs, then relax, then close again. To slow down, keep your legs close to his sides, resisting forward movement.

Hands
Your hands on the reins help control and guide the pony. Your reins should not hang loosely or you will have no control, but do not grip them too tightly either. Try to "feel" the pony's mouth and give with your hands as he walks. To stop him, do not pull back; instead stop "giving" with your hands.

Seat and back
Let your hips and back follow the pony's movement; if you increase the pressure he will speed up, if you stop following his movement he will slow down.

Voice
You can use your voice in different ways. You can reassure him, urge him on, scold him or praise him. He may not understand all the words, but he will pick up the tone of your voice.

USEFUL TERMS
leading file – rider in front of the ride
change the rein – change direction
whole ride – everybody together
in succession – one at a time
transition – change of pace (upward to increase the pace eg walk to trot, downward to decrease the pace eg canter to trot)

YOUR PONY'S PACES

Your pony moves at four different paces: walk, trot, canter and gallop. Each one involves a different sequence of leg movements, so they all feel quite different when you are sitting in the saddle.

Before you move off, your pony needs to be standing square so he can move forward smoothly and powerfully. From the side, your pony should look as if he only has two legs! This is because both forelegs and both hindlegs are lined up. His back legs should also be tucked underneath him. If one of his hindlegs is not square, use your leg gently on that side to ask him to bring it forward.

WALK

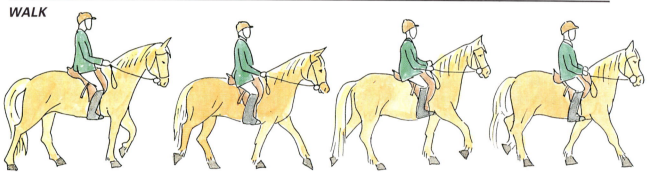

Walk has a four-time beat. The legs move in the following order: near hind, near fore, off hind, off fore. Shut your eyes and feel the rhythm. Walking speed is roughly 5–8 km/h. A sluggish pony may need more leg pressure. If he is moving properly he will be "tracking up" (placing the hind leg into the print left by the fore leg in front). You will also feel his head moving up and down as he moves along. Hold the reins lightly so your hands can follow the movement.

TROT

Trot has a bouncy two-time beat in which the pony moves its legs in diagonal paces. The off fore and near hind move together and the near fore and off hind move together. A pony trots at about 8 km/h. The rider can either rise in the saddle in time to the beat or sit and absorb the bounces. Both feel uncomfortable to start with! The rising trot is used most often; it is less tiring for both pony and rider. Rise forward slightly, then move back gently into the saddle.

To trot, close your legs quickly and lightly on your pony's sides and shorten the reins a little. Then close your legs more strongly against his sides. Sit for the first two strides to establish a steady trotting pace. You will rise and fall with the hoofbeats of the same diagonal. To avoid additional strain on his back, change diagonals occasionally; simply sit in the saddle for two beats then rise on the other diagonal.

USEFUL TERMS
off fore – right foreleg
off hind – right hindleg
near fore – left foreleg
near hind – left hindleg
left rein – moving anti-clockwise
right rein – moving clockwise

CANTER

Canter is great fun. You will feel as if you are moving very fast (about 16km/h). It has a three-time beat so there are three hoofbeats to every stride.

If your pony is cantering in a circle, he should lead with the inside leg otherwise he will be completely off-balance. Look down from the saddle to check the inside foreleg is moving before the outside leg.

To canter, close your legs, shorten the reins and sit down in the saddle. Then ask your pony to bend to the left or right. Push your outside leg back to ask him to "strike off" with his outside leg. Keep your inside leg firmly against the girth. The first time you canter, hold on to the front of the saddle if you feel insecure. Keep the canter going by using your legs and pushing forward with your seat.

GALLOP

Gallop is very fast: you may be travelling up to 40 km/h! You will not be allowed to gallop until you have become a safe and competent rider. Your pony needs to be fit, too. If he is not, you can harm his legs and "wind" (lungs). Your instructor will choose somewhere very safe for your first gallop. There should be no obstacles in the way and plenty of room at the other end to slow down!

You will need to shorten your stirrups slightly before starting. Then ask your pony to canter and use your seat and legs to drive him on until you achieve a longer, faster stride. When you are galloping you need to lean forward slightly out of the saddle so you take your weight off your pony's back onto your knees and the stirrups. Keep your legs against his sides and your heels down. The hands are held forward so the pony's neck can stretch out.

To slow down, press both legs against his sides and sit up. In this position you can give much stronger signals to your pony.

IMPROVING YOUR TECHNIQUE

SCHOOLING YOUR PONY

Once you have moved off the lunge rein, you are responsible for controlling your pony. To improve your riding, you will practise in a manège or schooling ring – either indoors or in the fenced off corner of a field marked out with straw bales. Ideally, the enclosed area should measure 40 × 20 metres and the ground should be flat. Although the manège is an oblong shape, you actually ride round it in an oval, so your pony bends round the corners. This increases his suppleness and improves your balance. As well as riding round the outside of the manège, you will progress to riding 20-metre circles and then to figures-of-eight.

To ride a circle, make full use of the width of the manège. Move your inside hand away slightly from your pony's neck to indicate the direction you want to go. Your outside hand stays close to your pony's neck to prevent him from bending too far and to control his speed. As with canter, pressure from your inside leg will signal the pace and encourage your pony's body to bend, while your outside leg stops your pony's quarters from swinging out. It requires considerable skill to give all these signals correctly. If they are too weak your pony will wander off the circle; if they are too strong he will overbend and become unbalanced. As you ride the circle, you should just be able to see the corner of your pony's eye.

MANÈGE ARENA
Above: Some of the exercises that can be carried out in a manège. Practise turning corners and riding diagonally and in circles – at all paces.

Below: The whole ride is exercising in a circle. Remember to keep the length of a pony behind the rider in front. If you are any nearer you will crowd her pony and may get kicked.

EXERCISING AT HOME
There are lots of things you can do at home if you want to become a fitter, more supple rider.

In the saddle
Stand with your feet about 60 cm apart. Bend your knees and bounce gently up and down. It's a bit like pretending you are on a steep ski slope, only your legs are much farther apart! This is your position in the saddle. You should not be stiff; your ankles should absorb the movement.

Sit-ups
An exercise for stomach muscles. Lie down and sit up with your arms folded. Get someone to hold your ankles or hook your feet under the bed or settee. Repeat six times. Increase gradually to 20 times.

Waist stretch
Put your right hand on your waist. Cross your left arm so your hands touch, then stretch them both out to the side, leaning over as you stretch. Repeat ten times then change arms.

Seat strengthener
Kneel on the ground. Bring your left knee up to your forehead, at the same time tuck your head into your chest. Then swing your leg up and out and stretch your neck so you are looking towards the sky. Repeat five times. Change legs. Build up to ten times.

Leg stretch 1
This is a useful exercise if you have trouble mounting. Put one foot on a fence, the other on the ground, slightly turned out. Lean forward over your raised foot, then straighten. Repeat with the opposite foot.

Leg stretch 2
Bend your left leg and place your hands on the floor either side of your foot. Stretch your right leg out behind you. Bounce gently up and down, then hold the stretch. Repeat with the opposite leg. Bring your outstretched leg up so it is level with the other one. Straighten your knees, then walk your hands away from you so they are at an angle of 45 degrees from your body. Lift your left and right heels off the floor alternately. This stretches your hamstring muscles.

Pigeon toes
A stretching exercise to help you sit deeper in the saddle. Stand against a wall and turn your toes inwards. Hold for ten and relax. Repeat.

Other exercises
Try skipping to develop your co-ordination and reflexes, and swimming to increase your lung capacity and stamina. Both are excellent ways to get fit.

LEARNING TO JUMP

Jumping is one of the most exhilarating riding activities. However, it is a mistake to try jumping too soon. You first need to have developed good balance and control.

Your instructor will lay out a row of trotting poles on the ground. You need to concentrate on keeping a good rhythm as your pony walks and then trots over them. Your pony's stride will shorten as he goes over them and he will also stretch his neck.

Above: Start with a single trotting pole and walk over it calmly. The instructor will gradually add one pole at a time so you are walking and trotting over a line of five or six.

Give with your hands when he does this. Always aim for the centre of the pole and turn smoothly at the bottom of the line. You may carry out this exercise in walk, trot and canter. Make sure you let your pony relax and stretch his neck afterwards.

Above: As the horse jumps, the rider needs to lean forward and give with his hands to stay balanced. Practise this position while your horse is standing still.

SMALL JUMP

Your instructor will next place a small cross-pole at the end of the line of trotting poles. The cross will encourage your pony to lift both front feet evenly. It also makes it easy for both of you to see the centre of the jump. That is what you should be aiming for!

By approaching it down the line of trotting poles you should be balanced and your pony will have a rhythmical, bouncy stride. Try to go over with your pony. Do not lean too far forward or you will catapult over his head if he stumbles or stops. On the other hand, try not to get left behind or you will throw him off balance, jerk him in the mouth and hurt his back when you land back in the saddle with a thud.

JUMPING POSITION

Try to look up and ahead as you go over the jump. Do not look to either side or you will become unbalanced. Keep your legs close to your pony's sides. Do not grip too hard with your knees; instead let your weight move into your knees and ankles. Your stirrups should be two or three holes shorter than for riding on the flat. You need to fold the top half of your body forward and move your hands forward to follow the horse's neck as he stretches it out. To start with, you will be jumping small obstacles and will not need to fold forward very far. As the jumps get bigger, however, this angle will increase. On landing, you slip back into the saddle and return to the normal riding position.

Once you have mastered the cross-pole you will move on to a small course of two or three fences and then to a combination (two or three obstacles placed close together). As you become more experienced you will learn to judge how many strides there are between fences and to feel your horse lengthening his stride in preparation for take-off. You need to learn how to keep in balance with him all the time – and this takes years of practice!

Below: 1 As you approach the jump keep your legs on your pony's sides to bring his hindlegs underneath him. 2 As he takes off bend forwards. 3 The moment of suspension over the jump. Look ahead. 4 The pony's forelegs touch the ground and he lifts his head and neck. Land gently in the saddle. 5 Sit up, collect yourself and ride on.

FEEDING

Above: Weighing out a pony's feed.

RULES OF FEEDING

1 Feed little and often It is better to give three small feeds a day than one big one; a big feed is harder to digest.

2 Feed according to a pony's needs This depends on his size, condition, temperament and workload. Most ponies eat about 1 kg of food for every 45 kg of bodyweight, so a 12.1 hands high pony weighing 212 kg will need 4.7 kg of feed each day. This is divided into hay, grass and concentrates according to how much work he is doing. Never try to work out a feeding programme on your own; always ask an expert for help.

3 Give good-quality food If you give him old, mouldy food he will get a cough, colic or stop eating. All ponies need fresh hay, succulents and a salt and mineral lick.

4 Feed plenty of roughage Roughage (grass, hay and straw) keeps the digestive system working. It also keeps a pony warm while it is being digested – essential in winter – and eating it stops a pony from getting bored.

5 Provide clean water Eating dry food makes a pony thirsty. Make sure he has fresh water at all times.

6 Water before feeding Encourage the pony to drink before a feed. If he has a large drink after eating he will wash the food out of his stomach before it is properly digested.

7 Do not work a pony straight after a feed Allow at least half an hour. A pony's stomach is close to his lungs. When his stomach is full he will not be able to use his lungs properly if he has to work hard.

8 Feed something succulent every day Ponies enjoy fresh, juicy food such as spring grass, apples, carrots and swede (in slices).

TYPES OF FEED

Horse and pony cubes: *these contain many ingredients compressed together. They are full of protein and can provide the basis of a healthy diet.*
Coarse mixes: *a mixture of ingredients eg oats, barley, flaked maize, crushed peas in chunky flakes.*
Oats: *an energy-giving food. They can be too "hot" for many ponies making them excitable.*
Barley: *slightly more fattening than oats but provides less energy.*
Flaked maize: *an energy-rich food especially good in winter.*
Bran: *already contained in cubes and coarse mixes. Do not give too much as it is fattening and bad for any pony.*
Hay: *sweet hay is the basis of a pony's diet. It is at its best between six months and a year after it has been cut. Dusty hay must never be used.*
Chop/chaff: *hay and/or straw cut into one-inch pieces. Encourages ponies to chew their feed properly.*
Carrots and apples: *succulent foods should always be given to stable animals. Slice lengthways; do not feed in chunks which can cause choking. Turnips can be left in the manger overnight for chewing.*
Sugar beet: *must be soaked for 24 hours before feeding in twice its volume of water – otherwise it will swell inside the pony and may kill him. Sweet and tasty.*
Molassine meal: *black treacle with a peat base. Adds sweetness and taste.*
Salt/mineral licks: *provide valuable minerals and vitamins. Ponies can lick them freely.*
Water: *should be available at all times.*

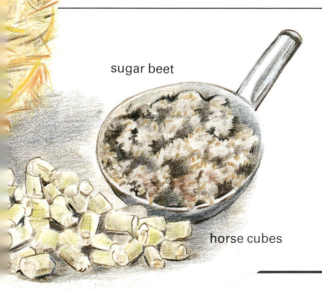

sugar beet

horse cubes

Above: Mucking out a stable.

HOW TO MUCK OUT

Every morning stables need to be mucked out. This means replacing the wet, dirty bedding with clean, fresh bedding. First tie up the pony with a quick release knot (see page 28) so he is safe and cannot escape. Put the wheelbarrow in the doorway. Remove the water buckets. Separate dirty bedding from clean with a fork. Using a shovel, move the droppings into the wheelbarrow. Shake the bedding lightly so the wet straw falls on the floor and toss the clean dry straw around the edges of the box. Sweep the dirty bedding into a pile and put it in the wheelbarrow. If woodshavings are used, you will need to cut out the dirty area with a shovel.

Spread the dry straw or woodshavings over the stable floor before you add fresh straw or woodshavings. Toss new straw and shavings with a pitchfork to separate them. The bed should be piled higher at the walls (30 cm) than at the centre of the box (22 cm) to stop the pony from getting "cast" (so close to the wall he cannot get up). Clean the water buckets, fill and replace. Remove the wheelbarrow, then untie your pony. As a healthy pony produces about eight piles of droppings each day, you will need to "skip out" (remove the droppings) several times a day.

TYPES OF BEDDING

Wheat straw makes the best bedding material; however, it can be expensive. Alternatives include woodshavings, shredded paper (good for ponies with breathing problems) and peat.

GROOMING

Grooming keeps a pony clean. It also stimulates the blood and tones up the muscles, helping to keep him fit. Grooming also prevents skin disease – ponies that are kept stabled must be groomed every day.

A BASIC GROOMING KIT

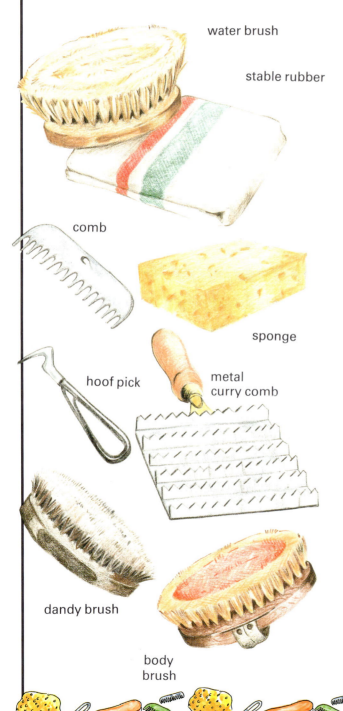

HOW TO GROOM
A grass-kept pony

You should not spend too long grooming a pony that lives out. In winter especially, essential oils and extra hairs in the coat provide warmth and keep out the rain.

If you are going to ride, brush off excess mud, especially round the saddle and bridle areas. If you do not do this, rubbing will make the pony's skin sore. Pick out the feet carefully; you should do this every day whether or not you are riding. Sponge eyes, nose and dock.

After riding, make sure the pony is dry before you turn him out again. Walk him to cool him down and groom off any sweat marks. A sweaty horse will catch a chill in winter and may get sunburnt in summer.

A stabled pony

A stabled pony should be given a quick brush-off before he is ridden and be groomed properly after exercise. Tie up the pony.

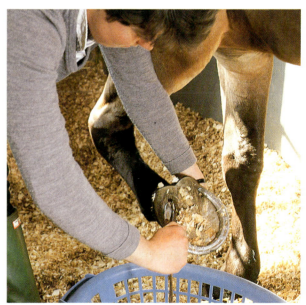

Above: Ponies should have their hooves picked out every day. Work from heel to toe, picking out mud and stones wedged in the foot. To make the hooves look black and shiny and keep them healthy, coat the hooves with hoof oil using a small paint brush. Always check a pony's hooves under adult supervision.

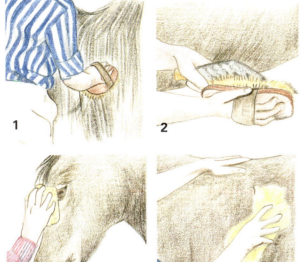

Above: A stabled pony must be groomed daily. 1 Pay good attention to your pony's mane and tail. 2 When using the body brush, don't forget to clean it through with the curry comb every six strokes. 3 Use a sponge to wash eyes, nose and mouth. 4 Finish off with a stable rubber.

of keeping a stabled pony warm at night. Modern quilted rugs also serve the same purpose. A sweat sheet is a cotton, open weave rug put on a pony after strenuous exercise to absorb sweat and a cotton summer sheet keeps flies away and ponies clean when travelling to shows. The rugs are kept in place by a roller or straps.

Undo any rugs. Remove stains with a water or dandy brush. Start on the near side of the pony behind his ears. Work down his body, using the body brush. Every six strokes take the brush over the curry comb to remove grease and dirt. Knock the curry comb on the floor. Cover the whole body, then change sides.

Groom his mane and tail. To groom the tail, hold it in your right hand and lift it away from the quarters. Gradually release small sections from your hand and groom these thoroughly with the body brush. Wash eyes, nose and mouth with a damp sponge and use a different one for the dock area. Groom the head very gently. Wipe over with stable rubber to remove last traces of dust.

RUGS

New Zealand rugs keep ponies dry in the field. Day rugs are heavy woollen rugs used on stabled ponies during the day; jute rugs, lined with a blanket, are the traditional way

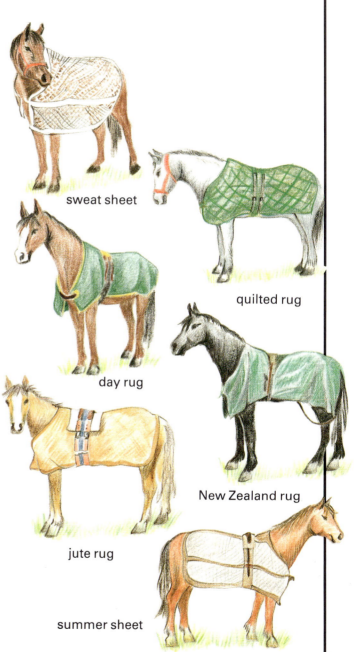

Above: Ponies need a variety of rugs throughout the year.

TACK 1

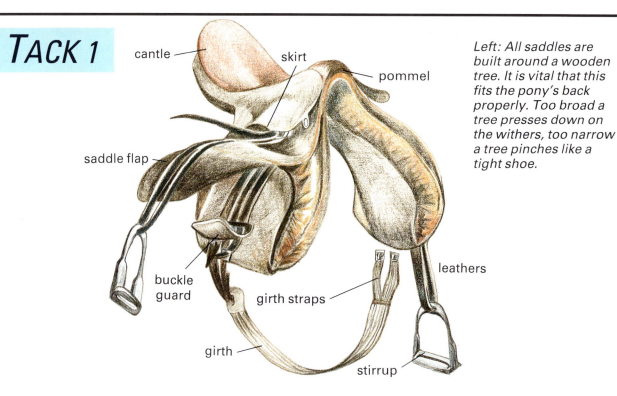

Left: All saddles are built around a wooden tree. It is vital that this fits the pony's back properly. Too broad a tree presses down on the withers, too narrow a tree pinches like a tight shoe.

If you visit a tack shop you will see a vast array of tack and equipment, yet it is surprising how little of it is actually necessary for the average pony. The two basics that every pony needs are a saddle and a bridle.

SADDLE
There are three main types of saddle: dressage, jumping and general purpose. You will need a general purpose saddle – designed, as the name suggests, for different types of riding activity.

GIRTHS
The girth is a strap designed to hold the saddle securely in place. The cheapest girths are Lampwick and nylon string girths. String girths are machine washable but when you fasten them you must check you are not pinching the pony. A wrongly-fitted girth will give a pony "girth galls". Leather girths are strong and long-lasting but must be kept soft and supple. They may be shaped, straight or crossover. Balding girths are narrower in the middle so they are less likely to rub.

COMMON GIRTHS

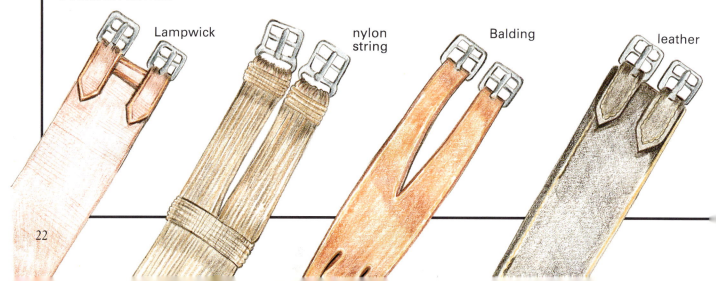

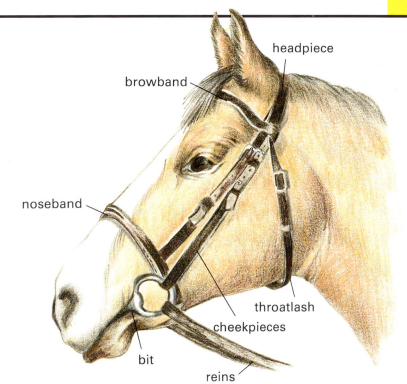

Right: This standard bridle has a cavesson noseband and a snaffle bit. The bit is thick and gentle on the pony's mouth. There is a wide variety available but some are very severe and will cause great pain in inexperienced hands. There are also many types of noseband which are used on ponies that can be difficult to control.

BRIDLE
A snaffle bridle is the simplest bridle and the most widely used by novice riders. It has a simple snaffle bit and a cavesson noseband. A double bridle, with two bits and two sets of reins, is used for extra control in dressage competitions and a pelham, with two reins and one double action bit, is sometimes used by advanced riders on very strong ponies.

BITS
There are hundreds of different types of bit available, but do not be in too much of a hurry to change bits if you are having problems controlling your pony. A pony's mouth is very sensitive and some bits, in rough hands, can kill the sensitive nerve endings in a pony's mouth and cause callouses. If you cannot get your pony to respond to your hands, check whether you are sending him the correct signals.

The most common type of bit is the snaffle. It works mainly on the corners of the mouth and on the lips. Jointed snaffles also put pressure on the tongue.

NUMNAH

You may have a numnah under your saddle. This is a saddle-shaped piece of stuffed cloth which fits underneath the saddle. Check it is pulled up inside the arch and that is is large enough to show all round the outside of the saddle.

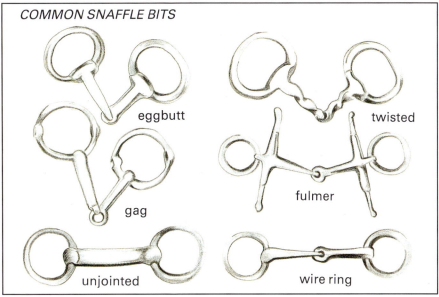

COMMON SNAFFLE BITS: eggbutt, gag, twisted, fulmer, unjointed, wire ring

TACK 2

PUTTING ON TACK

"Tacking up" means putting the saddle and bridle on a pony so he is ready to ride. You should always tack up in a stable at your first attempt so the pony cannot escape!

FITTING THE BRIDLE

First put the reins over the pony's head. Some ponies lift their heads, so you may need to use your left hand round his nose to guide his head down. Hold the bridle with your right hand and guide the bit into the pony's mouth with your left hand. Slip the bridle over his ears and pull the forelock through from under the browband. Fasten the throatlash and noseband.

There should be room for four fingers between the throatlash and your pony's cheek. The noseband should fit more snugly – there should be space for two fingers between it and the pony's nose. There should also be space for two fingers between the noseband and cheekbone above. The headpiece or browband should not pull and the bit should be roughly 12 mm wider than the pony's mouth. It should just wrinkle the corners of the lips. If it does not do this it is too low in the mouth; if it is too high it will pull the lips back in a grimace.

FITTING THE SADDLE

Stand on the pony's nearside. Place the saddle gently on his back and forward on his

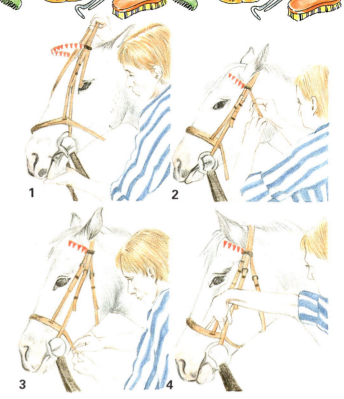

Above: Fitting the bridle. 1 Putting on the reins. 2 Fastening the throatlash. 3 Fastening the noseband. 4 Checking the fit.

withers, then slide it carefully down into place. This ensures that all the hairs of the coat lie smooth and flat. Lift the girth down (it should be folded over the top of the saddle, attached to the offside). Make sure it is not twisted before doing it up on the nearside. There will be two buckles, although most saddles have three girth straps. Do it up on the first and third straps.

When you are ready to mount, check the girth again. Do this gently and you will find it needs tightening. If you are rough, your pony will puff himself out so you will not be able to move it. However, as soon as you put your weight in the stirrup you will find the saddle has turned round and is hanging upside down under the pony's belly! Stretch each of the pony's forelegs forward before you mount to make sure the skin is not pinched.

Left: Putting on the saddle and doing up the girth.

CHECK THE FIT

When the saddle is on your pony's back it should not touch his spine. Any pressure will restrict his movement and give him nasty sores. Once you are in the saddle, you should be able to fit two fingers between the front arch and the wither. Someone standing behind you should see daylight from front to back between the saddle and the pony's back; but the saddle should not be perched on top, rocking you to and fro.

Correctly fitted saddles are very important. Ponies are all different widths, shapes and sizes. A narrow saddle on a wide pony will rub and a wide saddle will push the rider's weight onto the pony's loins.

Below: A well-equipped tack room. Tack should be cleaned every time it is used.

CLEANING TACK

Tack is expensive and must be cleaned after every ride. Hard, dirty tack is dangerous; it could break and cause a serious accident. A stiff saddle and girth will rub a pony's back and belly to cause sores and a dirty bit will make his mouth sore.

Ideally you should take the bridle and saddle to pieces when you clean them, but make sure you are with someone who knows how to put it all together again. Use a damp sponge to wipe the leather, removing dirt and sweat. Rinse and dampen the sponge, wring it out, then use it to rub saddle soap into the leather. Do not get the leather too wet. Oil it at regular intervals to keep it soft. Wash the bit and stirrup irons in warm soap and water. Rinse the bit – otherwise it tastes horrid! – then polish with a cloth.

BUYING/BORROWING A PONY

Your hobby has turned into an all-consuming passion and you feel it is no longer enough to go to the riding school every weekend – you want a pony of your own.

LEASING A PONY
More and more people are deciding that a leasing agreement suits their needs better than buying. If you lease a pony, you do not have to save up the money to buy him, nor do you have the problem of selling him once you have outgrown him. On the other hand, leasing can go wrong unless both parties are clear about just what is involved.

If you decide to lease a pony you must draw up a proper agreement. Think about all the points it should cover. These might include: How long will you keep the pony? How much notice should the owner give if he wants the pony back? Who is responsible if there is an accident? Who pays insurance? It is worth having the pony vetted before you sign the loan agreement. This will confirm that he is in good health.

If you decide to go ahead with leasing, have a month's trial period first. This gives you a chance to get to know the pony and the owners will be reassured that you are capable of looking after him. Then sign for a longer period.

BUYING A PONY
This is a tremendous responsibility and a costly one too. Before deciding to go ahead think about the following points:
Can my family afford it?
Apart from the initial cost of buying the pony you will have to pay regularly for the following: rent of a field or stable, feed and hay, straw, shoeing, vet's bills, tack, equipment,

WHAT TO LOOK FOR
Many experts look first at a pony's eyes. Are they large with a kind expression? Eyes spaced wide apart indicate a good temperament.

A well-proportioned head with alert, pricked ears is a sign of good breeding. A large head makes a pony unbalanced.

The neck should be firm and neither too short nor too long. A short neck can make the rider feel as if he about to tip forward. A horse with a ewe neck (this curves inwards between the head and body) is difficult to control as he carries his head too high for the bit to be effective.

Long sloping shoulders allow a horse to take long, flowing strides. A straight shoulder leads to short strides making the pony uncomfortable to ride.

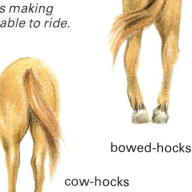

bowed-hocks

cow-hocks

Where to keep a pony

Ideally your local riding school would be the best place to keep your first pony. The experienced staff there will be on hand to help with any problems. Riding schools run several systems. These include: full livery – your pony is cared for completely and you are free to ride him whenever you can (very expensive); working livery – the school uses your pony for lessons, sometimes when you want to ride him! (cheaper); D-I-Y livery – you hire the stable and field and are responsible for caring for your pony totally (cheapest).

Living out

If your pony lives out you should check him twice daily to change his rugs, feed him and pick out his hooves; a stabled pony needs far more attention. Ideally your pony should be kept with others as all ponies enjoy company. His field must have proper shelter, secure fencing, good grazing (minimum of 0.8 hectares per pony), running water (a pony drinks about 35 litres a day), and be free from poisonous plants.

CHOOSING A PONY

What type of pony will suit you? Think about age, breed, size, temperament and conformation (build and appearance). Do not buy the first pony you see. Always take someone experienced to look at the ponies – your instructor would be ideal.

worming powders. It is impossible to put a figure on these costs, but your weekly paper round will certainly not cover the costs.

Can I look after it properly?

Your pony will depend on you for food, water, exercise, shelter, health and happiness. Can you make the commitment to visit him twice a day, seven days a week, to care for him? What happens when you are away on holiday or studying for exams? Will you know the warning signs if he is ill? Do you know enough about stable management?

A short back is strong but if it is too short it may restrict the horse's speed and he may hit his forelegs with his hind feet as he moves (over-reaching). The back should be slightly concave. A hollow back is a sign of weakness and possibly old age. A straight back restricts movement.

The chest should be deep and rounded. A wide space between the legs indicates plenty of heart-room and lots of stamina. The hindquarters should be strong and well-muscled.

The forelegs should be straight down to the pastern which should slope to the foot. Short pasterns give a bumpy ride, long ones are weak.

When viewed from behind, the hind legs should be straight, "cow-hocks" turn in at the points, "bowed-hocks" turn in at the toes.

The feet should face forward, be wide and open.

narrow chest

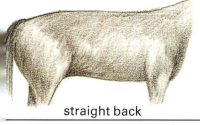

straight back

hollow back

WHAT NEXT?

Once you have been riding for a few months you may want to develop your hobby in other ways. Whether you are competitive or just enjoy testing your own abilities there is a wide choice of tests and competitions that will help you to develop your riding and stable management skills.

PONY CLUB

If you have your own pony it is well worth joining the Pony Club. There are branches all over the world. Rallies, lectures, demonstrations and Pony Club camp will combine learning to look after your pony properly and improving your riding with lots of fun.

Above: Pony Club mounted games are great fun but you need to practise the races beforehand so your pony understands what is expected.

QUICK RELEASE KNOT

Always use a quick release knot when tying up a pony. This is easy to do (see illustration). If the pony panics and pulls away you can release the knot by pulling the loose end of the rope. Do not forget to thread the end of the rope through the loop, otherwise the pony may undo it himself.

Right: Enjoying a riding holiday.

RIDING HOLIDAYS

There are hundreds of riding centres offering one- or two-week holidays in this country and abroad. You can opt for pony trekking through beautiful countryside on the back of a sturdy Highland pony, learn jumping, stable management or dressage skills, or decide that a fast, exciting trail ride is more your style. Some holiday centres organize lots of extra activities such as barbecues and swimming trips; others take you to different hotels along your route. The choice is tremendous; but standards also vary dramatically.

Before you book a riding holiday, visit the centre if you can. If this is not possible, send for a prospectus or phone to check that the activities are within your scope and a suitable pony will be available for you to ride. The holidays are advertised in all horse and pony magazines.

SAFETY ON THE ROAD

Always ride with the traffic and keep well to the side of the road but do not ride on the pavement. It is illegal. If you are worried by heavy traffic, stop in a nearby gateway. Walk and trot in a controlled manner; never canter on the road or even along the verge. Your pony could swerve out in front of a car.

Keep a length behind the pony in front; any nearer and he may kick your pony, any further and you will be dragging out the ride. Least experienced riders should always be in the middle of the ride.

To cross the road, wait until the traffic is clear in both directions, then cross in a straight line, very smartly. Always wear a riding hat or jockey skull cap. Never ride in fog or mist, or on icy roads.

A fluorescent jacket makes you more visible to drivers.

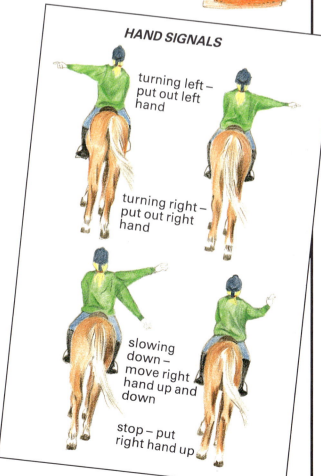

HAND SIGNALS

turning left – put out left hand

turning right – put out right hand

slowing down – move right hand up and down

stop – put right hand up

COMPETING

COMPETITIONS

Your riding school may let you hire one of the ponies to take to a local show – or they may hold their own gymkhana. Many weeks before a horse show takes place, the organizers will have produced a schedule of events and classes. Decide which classes you want to enter and check that you meet the entry requirements. When you first start entering competitions it is worth going along with other, more experienced riders from your riding school. They will help you enter for classes, collect your number from the secretary's tent, warm up and find the right ring – all the details you need to sort out if things are to go smoothly. Make sure you get to the show early and you know the rules of the competition in which you are taking part. Try to find a shady spot where you can tie up your pony when not competing. Remember your pony will require some hay or feed during the day and must have water.

There are many different competitive events. These are the most common:

Above: Show-jumping is very exciting. Before the competition you can walk round the jumps. Note the type and position of the fences, and the distances between them. You should jump the practise fence a couple of times to warm up your pony before he enters the ring.

Above: Your first show is a nerve-wracking occasion! Try to go with an experienced rider. You need to spend time before the show cleaning your tack until it shines and grooming and shampooing your pony. It is hard work but well worth it when you win a red rosette!

Gymkhanas – these are exciting games played on horseback. They include a version of musical chairs, an egg and spoon race, a contest to fill a bucket with potatoes, a bending race between a line of poles, a sack race with the rider hopping along beside the pony and chase-me-Charlie in which the riders follow each other over jumps that are raised after each round.

Shows – these range from small local shows to ones attracting top names in the showing and show-jumping worlds. There are usually classes for all types of ponies at all stages of training, for beginners as well as expert exhibitors. They include novice and open show-jumping classes; showing classes (ridden and in-hand) which judge conformation and performance, as well as the overall presentation of the rider; best rider classes; family pony classes for the good all-rounder; fancy dress, where the pony dresses up too; and possibly some gymkhana games.

Hunter trials – these are cross-country courses with "natural" obstacles, such as a stile, fallen tree, water jump, ditch, wood pile, bench and bank, some of which you may have to jump riding down a slope and some riding uphill. The jumps are marked with flags and jump judges record whether you clear each fence.

Dressage – the horse and rider perform a set of series of movements that are marked by judges. These test control, suppleness and obedience.

One-day event – horse and rider take part in dressage, show-jumping and cross-country tests that are held on one day. The rider with the lowest number of penalty points wins.

Long-distance riding – this is a growing sport that tests the endurance, fitness and stamina of both the horse and rider.

TRAVELLING TO A SHOW

If you are travelling to a local show make sure you leave plenty of time to hack there. You will need an adult to drive to the show with your tackbox, your pony's feed and your show clothes. However, if the show is some distance away, you will need to use a trailer or lorry. Your riding school should have one or, if a group of you are going, you may be able to hire a horsebox for the day.

There is a wide range of rugs, bandages and boots available for ponies to wear on journeys. These are necessary to keep him warm and to protect him from bumps and bruises while travelling. Leg protectors should always be used. Some types cover the knees and hocks too, so you do not need separate boots. You can now buy leg protectors that fasten with Velcro; this is much quicker than the traditional bandaging method. You must put on a tail bandage; this stops the pony from rubbing his tail against the end of the trailer. You can also get a special poll guard. This protects the pony's head from any knocks. Finally, he needs to wear a rug to keep him warm – in summer a summer sheet, with sweat rug underneath, will keep off draughts; in winter he needs a woollen day rug.

Below: Protect your pony from any knocks on the journey and provide a haynet to keep him occupied. Make sure you take all the equipment you need for the show.

INDEX

Aids 11, 23

Basics, mastering the 10–11
Bits, snaffle 23
Breeds of horses and ponies 4–5
   Arab 4
   Lippizaner 5
   Thoroughbreds 4
Bridle 23–5
   fitting/checking the fit 24
   parts of the 23
   types of 23
Buying/borrowing a pony 26–7

Canter 13
Cleaning equipment 25
Clothing 3
Colours of horses and ponies 5
Competitions 3, 23, 28, 30–1
   clothing for 3
   dressage 23, 31
   gymkhanas 3, 30
   hunter trials 3, 31
   long-distance riding 31
   one-day event 31
   showing 3, 30–1
   showjumping 3, 30

Exercising 11, 15
   at home 15
   in the saddle 11

Features of horses and ponies 5–7
Feeding and watering 18–19

Gallop 13
Girths 8, 22, 24
   adjusting the 8, 24
   fitting/checking the fit 22, 24
   types of 22
Grooming 20–1

Holidays 28–9

Illnesses 2, 20, 22–3, 25
   coughing and chills 2, 20
   girth galls 22
   mouth and saddle sores 2, 20, 23, 25

Jumping 16–17
   cross-poles, trotting poles 16–17

Knot, quick release 28

Lessons 2, 8–10
Lunge 10

Mounting and dismounting 8
Mucking out 19

Numnah 23

Pony clubs 28

Reins, holding the 10
Rugs 21

Saddle 22, 24–5
   fitting/checking the fit 24–5
Saddle, in the 9, 11
   controlling your pony 9
   exercising 11
   sitting correctly 9
Safety 9, 28–9
Schools 2, 4
Stables 19
Stirrups 8, 22, 24–5
Stopping 10

Tack 22–5
   fitting/checking the fit 24–5
Tack room 25
Technique, improving your 14
   manège arena 14
   schooling your pony 14
Travelling 31
Trot 12–13
Turning 10

Useful terms 11, 13

Walk 12

Published in 1990 by
Hamlyn Publishing, a division of
The Octopus Publishing Group Limited
Michelin House, 81 Fulham Road, London SW3 6RB

Copyright © 1990 Hamlyn Publishing, a division of
The Octopus Publishing Group Limited

All rights reserved. No part of this publication may be
reproduced, stored in a retrieval system, or transmitted,
in any form or by any means, electronic, mechanical, photocopying,
recording or otherwise, without the prior permission of
The Octopus Publishing Group Limited.

Illustrations: Sharon Gower, Joan Thompson

Photographic acknowledgements: Kit Houghton,
Bob Langrish, Octopus Group, Robert Owen

Cover: Bob Langrish, Gerald Whitcomb

ISBN 0 600 55542 9

Printed and bound in Italy